SUMMARY

OF

Final Battle:
The Next Election Could Be
the Last

By

David Horowitz

Max M. Ellis

Disclaimer:

You are viewing an **UNOFFICIAL SUMMARIZATION** of the content from the book "**Final Battle: The Next Election Could Be the Last**". The contents of the summary are not poised to replace the original book. It is meant as a complement to enhance the reader's understanding.

Once again, this complimentary guide intends to encourage the reader to get the original book to further their comprehension and understanding.

Copyright © by Max M. Ellis 2023. All rights reserved. Before this document is duplicated or reproduced in any manner, the publisher's consent must be gained. Therefore, the contents within can neither be stored electronically, transferred, nor kept in a database. Neither in Part nor full can the document be copied, scanned, faxed, or retained without approval from the publisher or creator.

Table of content

Book review

David Horowitz, who wrote "Dark Agenda," has a new book out called "Final: The Next Election May Be the Last." Indeed, it's fantastic! Get a hold of a copy. — PRESIDENT DONALD J. TRUMP I'm one of your biggest fans ever. For decades, David Horowitz has spoken the truth when practically no one else would.
Peter Hegseth
A "blueprint for the redemption of the United States of America," as the subtitle puts it.
By DENNIS PRAGER "Details the atrocities committed by the Biden administration and the Democratic Left." The Author, DINESH D'SOUZA

This is a dire prediction of what might happen if the current trend continues. Don't miss this! According to Peter Schweizer.

The Democrats have led the country down the road to a one-party state by relentlessly attacking the spirit of compromise that holds the union together. The real danger the Democrats pose to freedom is shown in Final Battle.

The heart of our democracy, the traditions that unite Americans, are in danger due to the development of socialism and critical race theory, as well as threats to the Electoral College, the Senate, an independent judiciary, and the integrity of the election system. Undermining the potential for bipartisan solutions to common challenges like viral pandemics and civil disturbances, attacks on these core American customs outlined by the Founding Fathers. The two parties are so polarized that the American way of life is in danger, and Citizens today talk in mutually exclusive political jargon. David Horowitz lays out the Democrats' signature tactics in a stunning expose of their evil goals: "Empires and states rise and collapse while everybody is watching." While onlookers may be caught off guard by the moment of collapse, in retrospect it will be easy to understand how everything came crashing down. Don't wait any longer to read Last Fight.

About the author

David Joel Horowitz is a prominent conservative policy advocate and writer in the United States. He also founded and still leads the David Horowitz Freedom Center and is the editor of FrontPage.

Horowitz grew up in a home with two communist parents. From 1956 until his total rejection of the Left in 1975, Horowitz was a vocal supporter of the New Left. Horowitz has written several retrospectives detailing his ideological development, with his 1996 memoir Radical Son: A Generational Odyssey serving as the capper.

Introduction

The October 31 campaign event for President Donald J. Trump was undoubtedly the highlight of 2020 for the 1,357 residents of Butler, Pennsylvania. More than fifty thousand people showed up to this tiny Steel Belt town airport three days before the election. The town is located 35 miles north of Pittsburgh. The crowd had gathered for Trump's fourth event of the day to hear his trademark brash delivery, sudden asides, and tired jabs at Joe Biden and the Democrats. They showed there to hear him repeat his pledge to restore America's glory, prosperity, and safety, and to yell "USA! USA!"

A Wall Street Journal reporter described Trump's final 17 hours of campaigning as "five awkward and hilarious stage dances to [the popular song] 'YMCA.'" Trump had travelled more than 3,000 miles in flights and motorcades, held rallies lasting 367 minutes in total, and performed "five awkward and hilarious stage dances to [the song] YMCA."

Trump rallies were always a good time to attend.

As has happened at previous demonstrations of this type the crowd eventually became so enthusiastic that they began chanting "We love you!" over and over again. Never mention that. If I start crying, it won't look good or me." It was an emotional outburst from Trump that showed a level of self-awareness and even self-deprecation that his many detractors failed to recognize.

The relentless candidate staged 45 rallies in the 21 days between his recovery from the Covid he had contracted at a White House gathering and the November election, with hundreds or possibly tens of thousands of supporters at each. On Election Day, Trump rode the presidential chopper back to the White House. About three in the morning, Marine One landed on the South Lawn.

Trump was so worn out when he got home that he missed his 7:00 a.m. interview on Fox & Friends by 45 minutes. After the concert, Trump spoke with a Pennsylvania radio DJ known for his conservative views. He told the interviewer, "These big numbers that are showing up to rallies are the ultimate poll." Nothing like it has ever been seen before.

Members of the Trump team gathered in the White House to watch the returns at 11:08 p.m. felt an immediate surge of optimism. The fact that Trump won Florida by a wider margin than he did in 2016 seemed to indicate that the balance of power in the battleground states had tipped in his favor. His pollster, John McLaughlin, had said he required 66 million votes to win; he was already on course to receive 74 million. The Trump team's confidence deflated, however, when 21 minutes later Fox called Arizona for Biden with barely 30 percent of the vote in.

Trump contacted his pal and Fox head Rupert Murdoch to pressure him into taking back the network's coverage of the election. To no avail, though. The next few hours were difficult for Trump as he tried to realize that the tide had changed and he was going to lose. He may take solace in the fact that he was still ahead in Pennsylvania by 690,000 votes. But a flood of late ballots was going to wipe out his lead there and in other swing states, and he didn't even know it. Trump fought back as media outlets pronounced Biden the winner based on partial election results.

On November 4, he told his supporters in a televised speech, "They're trying to steal the election." And we simply can't allow it to occur.... The election was actually a victory for us. Yet, there was an overwhelming amount of support for ensuring Biden's victory. Some senior Republicans were so worried about the fallout from a contested result that they proclaimed the election over. In the face of overwhelming opposition, Trump retreated to the White House, where he stayed mute for several days.

For the first time that week, President Trump left the White House on Saturday, November 7 to play golf at his club in Sterling, Virginia. He was on the seventh tee when he got a call from his son-in-law Jared Kushner, who informed him that the networks were ready to declare Pennsylvania a win for Democrat Joe Biden. With Pennsylvania's twenty electoral votes, Biden would have enough for a presidential victory. "Trump took the call calmly," an eyewitness said.

He had a casual conversation with his son-in-law while casually strolling through the grass, returned the phone to an attendant, and continued the final twelve holes while being followed by a caravan of twenty golf carts carrying Secret Service agents, law enforcement officials, and White House staff. Members of the club arrived while Trump was still on the course to cheer him on and inform him he had already won the match. Trump assured us, Don't worry. There is yet more to come.

Elections Matter

With a democracy that is grounded in the constitution, elections are a rite of passage. They recognize the will of the people as the ultimate authority, and they transform voting booths into the supreme tribunals of appeal.

When the American Republic was being established, its founders' greatest concern was the potential danger that would be posed by partisan divisions. They referred to the danger as a "tyranny of the majority," and they dreaded the possibility that the winning party would amass power in all facets of public life and utilize the authority of the federal government to force everyone else to live in a one-party state against their will. It is possible for democracy to be undermined from within by the tyranny of the majority. 1 The Founders of the United States of America set constitutional principles that were intended to force compromise and dampen the destructive passions that were released as a result of party agendas. They did this to prevent the United States from degenerating into a tyranny like that.

The concerns of the Founding Fathers led to the creation of a system of "checks and balances," which resulted in the separation and division of powers as well as the decentralization of authority. These measures were devised with the intention of thwarting the goals of the majority and restricting the governmental authority that it may potentially wield. Their Christian religion, which acknowledged that human people are flawed by nature and that their goals are not to be trusted, was mirrored in the skepticism and caution that the Founding Fathers displayed.

A state-based Electoral College, an independent judiciary with the ability to veto the wishes of legislative majorities, and a federal system that put both law enforcement agencies and voting regulations in the hands of the federal government were some of the provisions that the Constitution made to thwart unruly schemes. All of these provisions were included in the Constitution.

State legislatures rather than the federal government in Washington, District of Columbia, as the primary decision-makers.

The constitutional structure that the Founders constructed bestowed upon citizens freedoms that had never been seen before and were framed as limitations on the powers of the government. Their goal was to shield the people from the abuses of authority while also inspiring them to question conventional wisdom in all of its manifestations. They also arrived at a paradoxical conclusion. At the same time that the constitutional order decentralized power, it also served as a force that brought people together. Under the protection of electoral minorities, it was possible for the community of varied "voluntary associations" to flourish and thrive, as well as unite together as a single people to face the challenges offered by foes both at home and abroad.

The republic was meant to persist for as long as the concepts and procedures that were inscribed into the Constitution continued to be universally binding. The only battle in the nation's history of 250 years that was as intractable as the one pitting freedom against slavery was the one that tore the fabric of the country so severely and permanently that it led to a civil war. Compromise and prudence on our part were necessary to resolve the remaining disputes. In the event that one of their candidates did not win an election, there was always the chance for them to reorganize and win the election that followed.

Currently, the United States is dealing with a situation that many commentators liken to the start of the Civil War. One of the most prominent features of the fractures that currently exist in the body politic is the fact that all of the moderating institutions that were described above are currently under attack by the Democrat Party and the supporters of the Democrat Party. These institutions were designed by the Founders to soften the edges of political conflict and unify the nation. These include the Electoral College and the Senate, which Democrats want to do away with because they are "undemocratic;" the independent judiciary, which Democrats want to make an appendage of the legislative branch by packing the Supreme Court; the federal system, which reserves to the states rights and powers that are not specifically assigned to the bureaucracies in Washington; and the integrity of the electoral system, which Democrats refuse to protect by validating ballots through voter IDs.

Most dangerous of all, by insisting that the electorate be divided by race; demonizing their opponents as white supremacists and racists; and attempting to criminalize religious beliefs, Democrats have conducted a continual mug on the spirit of compromise that binds the merger together, and they have set the nation on the path to becoming a one-party state.

The Differences That We Face as a Nation

The traditions that unite Americans are in danger of being lost due to the fact that domestic factions are at odds with one another, in addition to the fact that institutions that keep the peace are under attack. They undermine the likelihood of finding solutions to common issues, such as pandemics and civil unrest that are acceptable to both political parties. The political discourse of the American people is currently distinct and antagonistic, and the two major parties are so ideologically opposed to one another that the voting process itself is under assault.

There have always been worries regarding the honesty of the voting process, but such worries had already reached a tipping point by the time of the presidential election in the year 2000 due to a contentious ballot count in the state of Florida. In the end, the case had to be brought before the Supreme Court so that it could be decided, and the court ruled in favor of the Republican nominee, George W. Bush, so crowning him the 43rd president of the United States of America. This electoral result was never accepted by the Democrats who were defeated; they referred to Bush as "chosen" rather than "elected," and hence as an illegitimate president because of this distinction.

This fissure in the body politic immediately led to an extraordinary about-face on the part of Democrats regarding their support for the war in Iraq in the year 2003. It was a conflict that George W. Bush had started, but Democrats were the ones who gave the go-ahead for it. It just so happened that a primary election for the Democratic nomination for president was going on at the same time as the United States was invading Iraq in the spring of 2003. As it appeared like an anti-war activist by the name of Howard Dean was going to run away with the nomination, Democrats as a whole turned against the war that they had authorized. There had been no significant changes on the battlefield to spark this new opposition. The Democrats rationalized their decision to switch parties by smearing the president, who, as a result of the contentious election in Florida, they already regarded as a political fraud. The Democrats argued that President Bush had misled the intelligence regarding "weapons of mass destruction" in order to trick them into supporting the war. This was done in an attempt to deceive them into supporting the war. Because Democrats who sat on the intelligence committees had access to the same material that Bush had relied on, this accusation was obviously baseless and should have been dismissed immediately.

But, this reality did not prevent Democrats from waging their presidential campaign in 2004 on the theme Bush lied, people died!—a slander that caused a rift between the parties that would have significant ramifications not only for the war but also for the political future.

Carter-Baker Commission Tries to Address the Issue

To address the issue that had so damaged American unity and the nation's ability to defend itself, former Democrat George W. Bush created the Iraq War.

President Jimmy Carter and former Republican Secretary of State James Baker joined forces. Together, Carter and Baker established the "Commission on Federal Election Reform." After a year-long study, they released a report with a number of suggestions to strengthen the electoral process's integrity and reunite the nation.

Among their key conclusions were recommendations to increase voter ID requirements; minimize the use of mail-in ballots, which "remain the largest source of potential voter fraud"; prohibit ballot harvesting by third parties; purge voter rolls of all ineligible or fraudulent names; and to permit election observers to monitor the ballot counting unhindered.

In 2019, a year before the Biden-Trump election, the nation was so politically inflamed that Democrats launched a massive campaign to modify the electoral regulations. They chose to do it in a manner that would reverse all Carter-Baker recommendations and facilitate election fraud. They rationalized their actions as measures to stop "voter suppression" based on race, as though blacks and other minorities were incapable of following the same standards as whites.

To enact their objectives, the Democrats filed close to 300 lawsuits, most of which were aimed at battleground states. The lawsuits were intended to extend the use of mail-in votes, weaken voter identification restrictions, legalize ballot harvesting by third parties, and legalize other practices that Carter-Baker had specifically tried to prohibit.

Three months before the 2020 presidential election, Democrats dispatched 600 attorneys and 10,000 volunteers to as many states as possible, including all battleground states, in response to the initial attacks on voting integrity. Their objective was to amend election rules by loosening and repealing safeguards that had been enacted to increase the process's security.

Trump Is Putting Up A Fight

Trump's response to the Democrats' assault on election protocols was to issue a warning via his Twitter account. He stated, "With Universal Mail-In Voting (not Absentee Voting, which is good), 2020 will be the most INACCURATE & FRAUDULENT Election in the history of the world." It will be a source of enormous shame for the United States of America." Then he threw forth the question: "Delay the Election till people can properly, securely, and safely vote?

It was a characteristic misstep. Trump was not authorized to postpone the election, but the hint that he may try to do so nonetheless fuelled the Democrats' persistent concerns that Trump would use his executive powers to prevent the election and remain in office permanently. Months ago his opponent Joe Biden had made exactly a similar charge: "Mark my words," Biden remarked in April. "I think he is going to try to kick back the election in some way, come up with some rationale why it can't be held," you said. "I think he is going to try to kick back the election somehow."

This was the case with the allegations that Bush had laid the excessively negative perceptions that Democrats hold of Trump led the supporters of their party to take such rumors seriously.

The significance of the new regulations was not lost on President Trump and his supporters. It was expected that the Democrats would make an attempt to steal the election. Polls showed that 61 percent of Democrats considered Donald Trump and his followers to be "racists," while 54 percent of Democrats considered them to be "ignorant." These results were evidence of how far factional fragmentation had progressed. 8 Their animosity for Donald Trump and those who supported him was so intense that they were willing to consider using any method at their disposal to remove him from office. On the other hand, there wasn't much that could be done to stop the negative impact that the new rules would have on Trump's prospects of winning. He didn't have much of a chance. He was compelled to observe, for instance, as Democrats in Pennsylvania, a vital swing state with 20 electoral votes, amended the election laws to favor themselves, despite the fact that doing so violated the Constitution of the United States. In doing so, he was in violation of the Constitution.

Under the United States Constitution, Article II, Section 1, Clause 2 makes it quite plain that the state legislatures are the only bodies that have the authority to establish the laws that govern elections. This provision was enacted with the intention of decentralizing and democratizing the voting process in order to counter any attempts by one party to seize power through institutions whose officials were not elected to their positions. In defiance of this unmistakable constitutional order, Democratic Legal Squads in Pennsylvania appealed their case directly to the State Supreme Court, where Democrats held a majority of five to two seats. This allowed them to circumvent the Republican-led state legislature and go straight to the state's highest court.

In response, the State Supreme Court, which is currently controlled by Democrats, has illegitimately authorized a number of new election laws that significantly favor the Democrats. As an illustration, the New York Times best-selling author Mark Levin provided the following explanation: "Just months before the [2020] general election, that court rewrote the state election laws to get rid of signature necessities or signature identical remove postal markings that were projected to make sure votes were cast on time and lengthen the counting of mail-in ballots to Friday at 5:00 p.m."

(The legislation of the state had established a firm day and time, and it was the previous Tuesday at 8:00 p.m Eastern Time) Election Day. To put it another way, the Democrats held the advantage which resulted in substantial changes to Pennsylvania's election laws and rendered the involvement of the Republican legislators in the federal constitutional process irrelevant.

10 The relaxation of the restrictions and the opposition of Republican poll-watchers made "ballot dumps" simpler which resulted in significant increases in the results of the election. At a Pennsylvania Senate committee three weeks after the election, sworn testimony was produced indicating that in one such dump, Biden earned around 570,000 votes, which is 99.4 percent of those cast, while Trump garnered only 3,200 votes, which is 0.6 percent of the ballots submitted. 11 The margin of victory for Biden in Pennsylvania was around 81,000 votes.

Trump's legal staff and allies filed 61 lawsuits in an effort to shut the stable door before it was too late. However, the judges practically never bothered to hear any of those lawsuits, and they were all dismissed from court.

They did so allegedly on procedural grounds, but it is more likely that they did so out of partisan prejudice or out of fear of the catastrophic ramifications to their institutions if they overturned the result of a presidential election. These same courts also rejected thousands of affidavits and declarations, the testimony of witnesses who testified in a variety of venues across the state, election analyses published by think tanks and legal centers, as well as video and photographic evidence of possible corruption in the process of counting the ballots.

The Highest Number of Votes Ever Cast

After the votes were tallied and the results were announced, two factors stood out as especially distressing for Trump. The first and most significant was his certainty that he had triumphed. Democrats and their media supporters had mounted a persistent smear campaign against him for more than four years, labeling him "worse than Hitler," a "white supremacist," a "sexist," a "racist," a "traitor," and even a "mass killer."

On the night of the election, Trump's presidential opponent, Joe Biden, made the latter claim. Biden charged Trump of killing every Covid-19 patient who died since the outbreak began in front of 70 million television viewers during the final presidential debate:

220,000 Americans were killed. If you only hear one thing from me tonight, let it be this: Anybody who is responsible for not taking control—indeed, anyone who does not proclaim, "I accept no responsibility,"

Last thoughts

nstead, he tells us that we are in the midst of a struggle hat, if we lose, would be our last. And he constantly eminds us that we are losing.

No, this is not a winning strategy. It's the anatomy of a tolen election, as well as the history of its effects. Iorowitz recounts the Left's efforts to discredit President Trump and the 74 million working-class Americans who backed him. This book describes in detail how Trump's extremist opponents did their dirty work, from unlawfully nanipulating voting protocols to launching a phony nsurgency on January 6, 2021.

Iorowitz presents the evidence in a severe and detailed nanner. It's all based on data obtained and spread by numerous media channels, from both supporters and detractors of Trump.

Iorowitz completely summarizes the situation:

Barbarian terrorist forces are already at the gates, and nside them, American leaders—military and civilian like—are concerned with delusory existential dangers ike climate change, white supremacy, and patriotic extremism.

The greatest grave threat to American democracy however, is the Democratic Party's drive to establish a one-party socialist state—a fascist state. This is evident in their assault on the First Amendment through so-called "cancel culture" and their complicity in the de-platforming of a US president and his 74 million fans.

They have advocated for the demise of the system of checks and balances that has served as the bedrock of American democracy for over 240 years. They have accomplished this by demonizing their domestic political opponents, attempting to abolish the Electoral College and pushing to abolish the filibuster and pack the Supreme Court; they have attacked the electoral system's integrity by opposing voter IDs; they have labeled anyone who questions election results as enemies of American democracy; and they have replaced America's liberating culture of individualism with a tribal identity politics that undermine the

Lastly, while delivering Islamic terrorists their most significant success since 9/11, they have worked to demonize and discredit their Democratic opponents as "domestic radicals" and terrorists. Their fervent support for socialist economics and political fascism puts us on the road to totalitarianism. All that remains at the end of these efforts are the gulags and deprogramming camps, which they openly promote."

Made in United States
Orlando, FL
06 May 2023

32876219R00017